A Dancer's Pocket Guide to
Embodied
Performance

A Dancer's Pocket Guide to
Embodied
Performance

Marcia Wardell Kelly

Epigraph Books
Rhinebeck, New York

A Dancer's Pocket Guide to Embodied Performance
© 2016 by Marcia Wardell Kelly

Design by Audrey Kelly & Colin Rolfe
Art contribution by Pacha Maia

ISBN: 978-1-9440-3756-7
Library of Congress Control Number: 2016962932

Author contact: *adancerspocketguide@gmail.com*

Epigraph Books
22 East Market Street, Suite 304
Rhinebeck, NY 12572
(845) 876-4861
www.epigraphps.com

Dedication

For those curious seekers and dreamers who find courage in the strength and reality of their imagination.

* * *

With gratitude, this Pocket Guide is dedicated to all of my teachers who planted seeds and gave me the encouragement and skills to tend them. Many thanks to dear friends and family who have supported my efforts writing this Pocket Guide. Special thanks to my husband, Jim Kelly, also a dancer, who helped me write this book.

Preface

This Pocket Guide takes an inside, experiential view of the art of dance performance. With it, I hope to encourage dancers to reach through and beyond technique into the rich landscape of expression that sensory embodiment allows. My goal is to help you develop your instrument and communicate material that deeply resonates within you and your audience.

I also invite readers who may not consider themselves dancers, but wish to gain insight into the expressive elements of the art, to join in the exploration.

I suggest that it be read in sequence as the ideas presented build upon one another.

Contents

Prologue

Carthage, Tunisia - July 6, 1972

We are standing in the women's dressing room—a staked out patch of bare stone set between ancient pillars. The local crew is wrapping this tiny space with a sheet of canvas. While they work, we neatly arrange our clothing and costumes on the backs of rickety folding chairs. We have water in a bucket and a lantern for light. In the twilight, stage lights are carefully focused, lighting cues set, and places marked with luminous tape. We manage to squeeze in a little time for a warm up and short run-through of the opening piece. We break a sweat and get our feet under us after the long bus ride from Hammamet where we last performed.

Make-up goes on quickly. We hear the audience arriving as we pull on our costumes as modestly as we can. The local back-stage crew takes their time as they randomly amble past our little dressing room, making privacy impossible.

The crowd sounds raucous and restless as they take their seats. We have no idea what they are expecting to see—or how they will view American Modern Dance.

We take our places in the ruins of the great Roman Amphitheater, the Mediterranean Sea at our backs. The sky is huge and pierced with stars. A breeze from the sea cools the desert air. It is a magnificent and magical place.

As touring dancers, we see the world through its theaters. Each venue presents a unique universe of its own. This Roman amphitheater is unlike the stately Teatro Colon in Buenos Aires with all the amenities of a glorious opera house. Nor is it the spare elementary school cafetorium in rural Alabama with its tiny child-sized bathrooms and hard tiled floors. This outdoor theater presents the open-air challenge of earth, sea and sky. A dancer could be overwhelmed by it.

What a responsibility it is for us to bring our dances to life here, in North Africa, amid the gravitas of space and time and history that this place contains!

It will take an enormous amount of focus to successfully perform in this setting. We dancers must be totally present now, in this space, in the elements of this place. Our most important work is to be aware—sensorially, physically, mentally, and spritually. Gathering our individual and collective energies, we transform them into living art. Embodying the choreography with energy and quality gives it a life force of its own. It speaks, filling the gap between stage and audience.

The first piece, full of rhythm and motion, breaks the ice with the pure audacity of its rhythmic base. The audience quiets down. The second piece is about time—slow continuous sculpture in motion. As I stretch open my chest, slowly arching back, someone in the audience cries out just as a shooting star tears open the night sky.

Now I truly know I am here. There is no place I would rather be—here in this timeless place, in my body, performing for this audience, right now.

Introduction

"Within the students' genes reside thousands of years of experience and knowledge; it is now their job to penetrate that wellspring of richness and to tap into what their bodies already know."

Murray Louis

It has been nearly 45 years since that evening in Carthage. The philosophy of embodiment that I practiced during my career as a performing dance artist informs all of my subsequent life's work and view of the world. I learned these principles from my teachers, Hanya Holm, Murray Louis, and Phyllis Lamhut. Performing under the direction of Alwin Nikolais capped my understanding of the philosophy in action.

Alwin Nikolais (1910-1993) was an artist ahead of his time. His theories of embodied dance performance represent a philosophical shift in dance art from narrative to abstract, and from centralized persona-dominated performance to an imaginative, spacious, and energy-filled experience grounded in the dancer's body.

In a nutshell, Alwin Nikolais taught dancers to sense elements of human expression by inhabiting their whole energetic physical instrument, being present in time, fueled by motion and shaped by enlivened space. By understanding the interrelationship of these and other basic elements, dancers can explore, create and express choreographic material with unique quality.

Our 21st Century Western culture is in the process of re-articulating much of what Nikolais so eloquently posed many years ago. Research in quantum physics, astrophysics, neuroscience, somatic studies, along with the widespread attention to the practices of yoga, meditation, indigenous healing systems and peak athletic performance all point to our current hunger and enthusiasm for embodied awareness—experiencing the sensory reality of being. This growing trend is encouraging and challenges the rising bodiless tide of information technology. As a culture, we seem to intuitively realize that we are missing something—something important. As performing artists—dancers in particular—

we can access and communicate what that "something" is.

Dance as an art form uses the medium of the human body. It is a temporal art, existing in a moment of unique communication between dancer and audience.

Live performance tests a dancer's mastery of the elements of the art. What is it that rivets an audience's attention to the subtlest detail? What quality of performance invites the audience to join with the dancer's physical exhilaration? What makes a performance multi-dimensional— simultaneously magical and visceral? How do we, as instruments of the art, prepare ourselves to skillfully meet these challenges?

Today's dancer learns a broad range of highly patterned skills. Technical mastery provides a base line of strength, range and facility. However, technique can also pattern the dancer's neuromuscular circuits in a way that can block or mask the potential for being present in the moment of performance. When technique serves only technical facility, fear of making mistakes or failure in execution can haunt a dancer who has not developed the creative tools to fully embody choreography.

Each chapter in this guide could yield many hours of improvisational exploration. Improvising challenges you to listen to your sensory body, allowing it to speak for itself. It is an invitation to become acquainted with your body's intrinsic creativity.

Whether you are exploring this broader territory on your own or with a teacher, the concepts in this guide will provide you with ground for experimentation.

As a performing dance artist, you are already aware of your responsibilities to the choreographic material, to your audience and to yourself. You understand the need to communicate a clear view that resonates with your audience. I am going to ask you to delve deeper into the creative experience that embodied dance performance offers.

Pause occasionally as you read this guide. Allow your body and your imagination to open as you explore, practice and integrate the processes presented. It is my hope that this perspective will assist you to further develop your personal relationship with the art of dance.

Let us begin.

Surrender of
"Command and Control"

"Performing makes high demands on the human ego. Yet, the artist must go beyond himself. Great performers are willing to transcend themselves to live within the substance of their art."

Alwin Nikolais

As dancers, we sometimes mistakenly allow the vital energy of our bodies to conform only to our emotions and thoughts, which by their nature are limited and pre-conditioned. When this occurs, we block from our awareness the enormous amount of sensory intelligence provided by the body as a whole.

One of the most important contributions to the language of dance performance is Alwin Nikolais' concept of decentralization.

Decentralization is a somatic discipline. Its practice trains the dancer's mind to merge with the sensing body in service to the choreography rather than to the definition of the dancer's personal identity.

In a psychological sense decentralization surrenders the "command and control" function of the mind – with all its patterns and stories, to full partnership with the body's geography. In return, the body is freed to feel and experience the totality of the present moment. The mind can thereby follow the body's lead through an ever-changing perceptual field.

Dancers explore this vast territory through improvisational problem solving. Improvisation invites the dancer to create a partnership with imagination and intuition, trusting the body to make split-second decisions based on the immediacy of sensory input and motional output. The embodied nature of improvisation translates into decentralized performance.

To the decentralized performer, choreography provides a roadmap to be perceptually traversed. The process of decentralization disables the habitual overlay of inhibition, exhibition, judgment, pre-conditioned movement patterns, and over-thinking. Now, through the dancer, the choreography speaks for itself.

The first task for the student is to become acquainted with their sensory geography.

Try this:

Find a quiet spot on the floor to lie down on your back cushioned by a blanket. Close your eyes, quiet your breathing and allow your body to sink into the floor.

Use your imagination to lead your mind's eye on an internal body scan—taking a sensory inventory of your body.

Very slowly and deliberately, focus on your right foot: sense its size, volume and all the variety of sensation that you can harvest (examples: temperature, contact with floor, weight, tingling, pulse, involuntary movement, etc.).

In the same fashion, explore each toe, the bones and flesh of the foot, the ankle, the lower leg, knee, thigh and hip. Repeat on the left side.

Next, explore the pelvic bowl, the individual bones of the spine and ribcage, the abdominal organs as well as the rhythms of the lungs and heart. Especially feel the back surface of the body's weight against the floor. Continue through the right shoulder blade and shoulder, upper arm, elbow, lower arm, wrist and individual fingers. Repeat on the left side. Now feel the upper spine, neck and skull. Continue surveying the substance of the head and the sensory organs it contains. Feel the weight of the head sinking into the floor.

Envision the entire internal space of the body. Feel the body's interrelated wholeness, its breath and moving energy. While maintaining this internal whole body view, slowly open your eyelids. Is it possible to maintain the interior sensory view with the eyes open? Are you able to come to a standing position while maintaining this view? Can you take a few steps? Can you lift your hand to touch a point in space outside your body and still sense your physical totality?

The Body View:

The above exercise is a first step in the process of embodiment. The ability to focus internally, constantly harvesting sensory information, is the equivalent to tuning a complex musical instrument. Your whole body is the instrument. Through it, the building blocks of dance— motion, space, shape and time—are projected and expressed.

In Performance:

During the hour prior to your performance, find a few moments to complete a quiet body scan or simply allow yourself to consciously rest. This will ground, balance and decentralize your energies as you mentally and physically prepare to perform.

Initiating Motion

"Dance involves the activation of matter in time and space, engaging gravity, centrifugal and centripetal forces, and the infinite inter-balances of all these relative factors. "

Alwin Nikolais

Movement is everyday action: making a gesture, changing locations or taking a position. Motion, on the other hand, is a dynamic state. Motion is how we sense, shift and transition as we move. Dancers are in an ever-changing process of creating, refining, qualifying and communicating as we dance. We learn how to decentralize while in motion, guiding energy through space and time in a meaningful way.

Four important and interrelated aspects of motion to explore are: Stasis, Impulse, Grain and Gravity.

Stasis

"The dancer bears within himself a potent force, the form of his own material presence."

Alwin Nikolais

The dancer's neutral is an enlivened condition. Nikolais calls this state stasis, the state of apparent stillness. However still it may seem, stasis is filled with vital energy, the dancer's entire body attuned. Stasis is fully embodied presence. It is without past or future and gives no clue to previous or following movement. Dancers learn to be fully present in space and time, especially while still, for it is within this heightened state of presence that the impulse for motion is born.

With strength of will and imagination, you create a vision of internal energy in motion. As a dancer, what you see and what you feel become one vision. This awareness is essential to your ability to create states of being. When you experience decentralized stasis, you become the expression of nascent dynamism—a state of kinetic potential, moving in all directions simultaneously, energy humming within your physical body ready to become something more.

Try this:

(1) *Stand at full height with feet hip width apart. Imagine you are filled with bright light. As if controlled by a dimmer switch, experiment with brightening and dimming the intensity of the whole body light. How does this change your perception of the size and consistency of your body?*

(2) *In the same standing position, feel the always-moving internal energy of the whole body and experiment with "standing still fast" or "standing still slow" or "standing ready in anticipation." How do these intentions change your perception of potential motion?*

The Body View:

The functions of the living body are never still. The brain and organs of digestion, circulation and respiration are always active. The heart is fed by the oxygen in our breath and rhythmically circulates blood throughout the body to every cell. All of these large systems are connected. It takes a unique quality of imagination and heightened physical awareness to transform this intrinsic physicality into the holistic state of stasis.

In Performance:

Engage in the state of stasis with an appreciation for its part in the broader scope of choreography. A choreographer will often ask you to simply be still or enliven the space for other dancers. Think of this as being, not waiting. It will better prepare you for your re-entry into the moving choreography.

Impulse

"To reveal the motion that exists in movement was to reveal the life force and gift of change that distinguishes the animate from the inanimate."

Murray Louis

An impulse is an internal kinetic command that organizes energy into action. It is the trigger that impels the matter of the body to change, to find itself in the state of motion. It may be a subtle release into gravity or a push against gravity. It may propel you into locomotion. Sufficient impetus will catapult you into the air. The important thing to remember is that you generate action with impulse.

Try this:

(1) *Stand in a state of neutral totality. Enliven your energy to a state of stasis. Continue in this state until you begin to feel an impulse to move arise. You may imagine yourself breaking into a run, dropping to the floor or lifting the arm in gesture. Do not act upon these nascent impulses. Observe what is happening in your body and mind. Disengage and return to a neutral state of totality.*

(2) *Now, stand again in stasis and as an impulse to move arises, consciously create the intention to go with it. Pull the energy trigger, propelling the dynamic impulse through its trajectory, ushering it to its dissipation.*

Experiment with the power of impulses, releases, propulsions, and outcomes. How does this range of energy affect the dynamic trajectory and outcome of each impulse?

The Body View:

As you feel the impulse arise, there is no pretending. There is a rising commitment to truly change state: to be and then become something else altogether. Choosing to release into motion invites the physical agreement of intention and sensory input.

In Performance:

As you warm up your body before a performance, use impulse to propel your energy into dynamic form. Instead of a executing a simple muscular warm up, identify the dynamics within each exercise. Now practice the exercise with impulse, trajectory and outcome. In performance you will be releasing and propelling your energy through the dynamics of a choreographic form.

Grain

"The dancer, by graining toward the intent of the movement, can direct the viewer's eye to the subtlety and direction of an action. He also makes visible the internal continuity and flavor of the choreography."

Alwin Nikolais

The word grain is used in the same way that the flow of wood grain is evidence of a tree's direction of growth. It is a clue to the tree's life force and intention.

When a dancer grains, energy moves through the body as if every cell in the organism knows where the dancer's mind is focusing. Graining spotlights this focus by simultaneously casting the body's full attention toward it.

Using another metaphor, grain is felt within the body like the irresistible pull of iron filings to a magnet. For example: when one's attention is pulled toward a specific point (on the skin's surface or within the body) the body literally pulls closer to the focal point to reveal it.

Dancers sense this process as a subtle plasticity. The body transforms itself to acknowledge and reflect its focus. The focus may be a still point or a motional flow. For grain to work, there cannot be conflicting signals or absentee body parts. The dancer employs whole body's intelligence and clarity toward its motional intention.

Decentralized energy constantly shifts with the help of impulse. By graining toward your motional intention, you begin to sense and control the moving energy. Your body learns to make split-second decisions based on the immediacy of sensory input and motional output. A new trust is actively built between your creative imagination and your body's ability to generate a dance as it unfolds. Although difficult to master, this allows you, as a performer, to own your whole body's experience.

Try this:

(1) *Begin standing in stasis. Keep the feet easily connected to the floor as you maintain your attention on your internal body space. Create and follow an internal impulse moving backward toward the lower spine. Envision this impulse as a tennis ball sized orb of moving energy. Feel the plasticity of your whole body as it moves to focus and grain toward the moving orb. Now, redirect the impulse forward through the torso to the upper chest and grain toward it as it travels. Move your feet only enough to accommodate the internal itinerary. Propel the point out the right shoulder and arm into a fingertip. Reverse the impulse, following it back through the torso, down through the pelvis into the left thigh, lower leg and foot, always graining the rest of your body toward it.*

Allow your whole body to feel the magnetic pull of the moving focal point and have a synchronous plastic relationship to it. Is there any part of you that is not attending to the moving point? Repeat several times, experimenting with the strength of impulse. Invent your own itineraries.

(2) *Another way to use grain is to initiate motion through space. Begin in standing stasis. Sense the surface of the body from head to toe. Feel how the surface of the body contacts the space in front of you.*

Imagine you are being pulled into your forward direction as you grain the entire frontal surface of your body toward forward space. Now, sensing the entire frontal surface of graining energy, release your body into the forward space walking quickly across the floor. Repeat the same process spotlighting different body surfaces and directions as you release forward, backward, sideways, diagonally, up or down. The ability to grain into release allows you to shift directions quickly without stopping. Explore and test the moment of release and directional change.

The Body View:

Eye focus can often dominate decentralized body focus and unconsciously work against the grain. Practice modifying your ocular focus— see how your vision can harden, soften, become peripheral, near or distant. Most importantly, try to recede back through the eyes into the body as a whole. Begin to "see" through every pore and cell. In this way, the eyes contribute to visual focus in balance with the whole body, not as the defining signal.

In Performance:

Your ability to grain is a gift to the audience. You are casting a subtle spotlight on how the dance is developing. Keep your focus relaxed and take the viewer with you on a guided tour of the choreography.

Dancing with Gravity

"You need gravity because it gives you the power. The challenge is to use it."

Hanya Holm

The force of gravity is a dancer's primary physical reality and our ever present dance partner, whether in stasis or in motion. Gravity is our connection to the earth, giving us the sensation and measure of our weight.

Gravity and the laws of motion are inseparable and together form the primary sensory basis for balance as well as the exhilarating experience of motion through space. Impulse impels the physical substance of the body into the state of motion.

You sense the effect of gravity on the contents of every cell and learn its value when you spin on a central axis, drop weight to the ground, lift weight into suspension above the ground, expand away from your center with centrifugal force or pull in toward your center with centripetal force.

Sensing gravity's pull opens us to the duality of up and down. Dancers love the journey between the poles of that duality: falling out of balance and rebounding to catch a balance again; using effort to push away from the pull of gravity then releasing to the ground; shortening the interval between push and release to vibrate and ride rhythms.

As you gain confidence partnering with gravity, you find poise in aligned balance. You sense the pressure of the foot against the floor as you leap beyond gravitational pull into a state of suspension and as your joints softly cushion your return to earth.

Without the intention to renew energy and impulse, gravity will eventually bring any motional impulse to ground. Being conscious of gravity allows you to catch your body's weight as it releases and transform it into momentum. Harnessing these forces in service to choreography leaves an audience catching its breath.

Try this:

(1) *Lie on the floor, back down, your body well cushioned by a blanket. Slow your breath and release your whole body weight into the pull of gravity. You do not need to exert any energy to hold your body in any form whatsoever. Note how much effort is needed to lift the ribcage as you simply fill your lungs with breath and how much you relax into gravity as you exhale.*

Sense the weight of your head against the floor. It is heavy—10 pounds on average. Test how much effort is needed to slowly lift and hold it one inch above the floor for 10 seconds. Slowly release your head back to the floor and relax into gravity.

(2) *Sit on a hard chair, your spine balancing the torso and head in the vertical, arms released down to your sides. Using the least amount of effort, take 60 seconds to simultaneously lift the extended arms up wide to each side (2nd position). Hold the arms in this position for 30 seconds. Abruptly release the arms and let them fall relaxed to your sides.*

(3) *Stand in the vertical with the right arm extended wide to the side. Feel the weight of the arm extended in space. As you release the right* *arm to gravity, catch the dropping weight before it dissipates, lifting the arm in an arc in front of you. Hold the arm in front, release the weight, catch it and ride the weight on an arc to the right side wide position. Release, catch, and ride forms the sensory basis for keeping mass in motion. Examples of this are fall and recovery, swing, rebound, rhythm and momentum.*

The Body View:

The body's center of gravity, generally located within the lower abdomen and pelvis, connects the full weight of the body to gravity. It is part of the central vertical core through which gravity aligns the body in balance - from the soles of the feet through the crown of the head. Consciously falling off balance or dropping from suspension into gravity initiates a rebounding arc of fall and recovery.

As you sense and understand how your body in motion partners with gravity, you will be able to extend out through the body and limbs, stretching away from the center of your body against the pull of gravity. Your extended body in motion fills space with energy and creates a stronger field of force.

In Performance:

Fear and anticipation quicken the pulse and breath. As your breath becomes shallow or if you hold your breath, your center tends to lift into the upper body. This unstable condition severs you from gravity's available power. Root your feet, breathe in through your roots and release your energy down into the earth as you exhale each breath. Now your center has grounded legs to stand on.

Motion

"The unique character of dance is that motion itself is the end; reason is within it rather than beyond it. Dance accomplishes itself."

Alwin Nikolais

Having explored stasis, impulse, grain and gravity, you now find yourself entering the main event—you are in motion. Embodied performance involves the conscious qualification of your physical, mental and subtle body energies in motion.

Being and staying in motion requires commitment. You manage and modulate how much energy is required to fulfill motion's many qualities: vibration, lyricism, percussion, force, rhythm, locomotion, rotation, swing, suspension, fall and rebound.

As you explore a broad range of motional qualities, you learn to develop a tangible sensory knowledge of each.

Try this:

(1) *In a large space, move continuously in any way you want. Never stop. As you tire, begin feel the efficiency of releasing weight into gravity, rebounding, falling, swinging, balancing.*

(2) *Begin to propel the body around the room utilizing different parts of the body to produce various impulses (examples: chest, hips, knees, shoulder). Note when the dying momentum of one impulse begs for the production of the next. Keep it moving.*

Increase the dynamic range of your impulses by utilizing opposite qualities (examples: soft/ percussive, fast/slow, heavy/light). Observe the difference in the duration that each quality of impulse produces.

(3) *Choose a specific joint action (elbow, knee, wrist, shoulder, hip, ankle, etc.) and use it to create a repetitive motional pattern (flex, extend, rotate, twist, etc.). Experiment with the detail and range of the motional qualities you employ as you perform each repetition.*

The Body View:

Dancers can underestimate the motional potential of the feet. We take their complexity for granted just because they happen to be at the end of the legs and take us where we want to go. Feet are more than merely functional. They are masterpieces built for strength, flexibility and motion. At the same time they are sensors sending vast amounts of information to the rest of the body about the terrain they traverse. Feel how they coordinate with the ankles, knees and hips to launch you into space in an infinite number of ways. Appreciate how they absorb the impact of meeting the hard surface of the floor, softening and quieting each landing.

The joints are keys that unlock and reveal the motional structure of the body. Each joint is nexus of energy, nerve and fluid circulation. Take your mind's eye into individual joints and explore the range of motion available within them. Kinetic energy produced during joint action can crackle, whistle or sing as it is transformed into dynamic motion. It can be immediate, like a startle or shock. It can be lyrically slow and elegant like a wave. Control these energies, so that they become the "verbs" in the basic language of your body in motion.

In Performance:

Don't be caught looking for your energy in the first act! In warm up, run, jump, spin, boogie—do what you need to do to get your energy moving. Ignite your motor base—your body's electrical, vibrational energy transformed into physical motion. Propel this energy forward into locomotion through space. Ride the resulting momentum's build and dissipation.

As you run through a dance before show time, break a sweat and find your breath. Rather than saving energy for the performance, create energy. Be ready to hit the ground running when the curtain rises.

Space

"When one is released from centralization, one becomes completely aware of an infinite environment."

Alwin Nikolais

Now imagine that you are a porous, space filled being. (You actually are!) You are not only skin, muscle, bone, organ and sinew. You are not only cells responding to electrical impulse. You are not only protons, neutrons and electrons. You are also the space in between.

Perceiving this internal space as contiguous with the external space beyond your skin connects you to all the energy around you as far as your senses reach. Once you have discovered the physical extension of inner space into space beyond the skin, you are able to see and work in a much larger field.

With this awareness of space, you step into the dimensional geometry of points, lines, curves, planes, and volumes. All of the moving particles of your decentralized, sensed space begin to re-align with whatever spatial aspect you intend to reveal or project. Aside from geometry, space has the qualities of texture, density and atmosphere. Space is the medium through which your motion reverberates and connects to your audience. You make space visible with your body.

As you work with space, the tactile senses become extremely important, especially when working in your peripheral space. The body becomes a paintbrush on a multi-dimensional spatial canvas. You reveal invisible spatial architecture and texture every moment your body physically touches it. Similarly, you feel the height and breadth of the space and calibrate your energy accordingly. Touch gives space consistency and visibility that communicates to your audience.

Try this:

(1) *Imagine your personal space as a spherical egg-like volume surrounding your body. Its outer limit is defined by your body's peripheral reach. Envision this spatial egg divided into three distinct levels: high, medium and low. Choose one point in space within each of these three levels. Be sure that the distance between the three points is far enough so that your body must stretch, twist and bend to reach them. Now, touch each individual point with your right fingertip. Then, in sequence, draw lines from point A to B to C to A. Try the same process with your right big toe, then the elbow. Experiment with other body parts. How must your body move to accomplish this?*

(2) *Can you see and feel space? Imagine that the space in your practice room is heavy and viscous like honey, or prickly, or filled with shards of glass. Without moving, can you see and sense it? How does that imaginary spatial texture qualify your action as you move through the space of the room? Try reflecting the outside spatial texture inside your body. How does this change the quality of motion of your inner space?*

(3) *Can you create a spherical volume by encircling it with your body or parts of your body? Can you create the same volume by placing your body or parts of your body in motion around the volume? Try this exercise with horizontal, vertical or tilted planes. Try the same with cubes. How does the shape of the space influence motion? Can you keep your focus on the space?*

The Body View:

Dancers sometimes block the energy flowing through the body by unconsciously shaping and hardening the hands. This blocks openness and inhibits release through the fingers into space. When you use the highly evolved tactile senses of the hands as a sensory model for the rest of the body, you gain access to a broad variety of tactile body articulation.

The feet are able to articulate well beyond the functional definitions of "pointing" the foot, full point, half-point and flexed. They are capable of extending energy beyond the leg into peripheral or linear space. Let the feet open to the flow of energy more like hands. Toes can see too.

Led by the sternum, the open chest is the center for experiencing the joy and exhilaration sensed while moving through space. Use your breath as a spacious energy moving into and out of your body as a whole. Take it in and open up to the space around you. See it all.

In Performance:

When you first enter a new performance space, survey its height, breadth, depth and unique architectural design. Look out and find the last seat in the top row, the seats close to the proscenium and to the side. These seats will be filled with people during performance. Practice modulating the energy needed to reach through the space to connect with the audience.

If you are outdoors, is the sky your roof? Define your boundaries. It is easy to become disoriented in such an open environment. When disoriented, the body tends to contract. Boundaries make your space manageable. Without them, you may lose the opportunity to reach out and contact your audience.

Shape

"In designing sculptural forms, the facility of the body is truly wondrous."

Alwin Nikolais

Shape is dynamic. Dancers' bodies move into and out of shapes in a myriad of ways. A shape can be a full bodied shape or formed with part of the body. In that way a shape can be static or can be transported, rotated or turned upside down.

Each armature of a shape represents potential motion. As key joints kinetically release that armature into motion, your shape may drop, swing, twist, spring or shatter. You may dissolve from one shape to another. You might find your body fitting into space as a hand fills a glove. You may take shape while in flight. You may be extending your shape through other dancers' bodies to create larger complex shapes. The shaping of your body never stops as you attend to the sensation of density and sculptural form when releasing into and out of motion.

Shaping the body requires an understanding of total density, solidity, volume and form. All of the unfocused energy within your body comes to a common sensory agreement and fills the inner body space with uniform volume. Every square inch of the skin feels the same internal pressure. This is a form of graining from the center of a shape out to the skin surface.

The internal volume of a shape may be empty or dense to the point of solidity. This qualification implies a sense of weight and influences how gravity forms and releases you from a shape.

Fully embodied shape is a decentralized condition. Sensory attention is dedicated to the realization of physical form in its totality. Shapes, when fulfilled by the dancer, shift into recognizable visual and tactile symbols— abstract clues and impressions leading the viewer to the glyphs of a fresh, new language.

Try this:

Create an unusual whole body shape that you are able to hold for an extended length of time. Sense that you have decentralized your focus and feel the consistency of the shape's inner density and the pressure it exerts against the skin from the inside.

Feel the surface definition of the shape and its impression in the space around it. Step out of the shape and look back to see where the shape existed in space. Step back into the shape and feel its wholeness and substance. This will help you sense and visualize the communicative power of shape.

Experiment with other shapes and their relationship to spatial volume and density. Go to a museum and view sculpture with a spatial eye.

The Body View:

Shape and space are bound in an intimate relationship. The physically aware body, when sensing its density is able to give consistency and volume to the space inside the skin. This inner three-dimensional volume becomes a legible shape when set into the mold of space outside the skin. The space around the body supports and reveals the body's shape. In its material form, the space within the body defines the shape of space surrounding it. Again, tactile senses come into play by creating sculptural surface definition at the skin's interface with surrounding space.

In Performance:

A performance can fly by in a flash. Take time to fully inhabit shapes—relish the novelty of each. Think volume and density. Avoid the risk of becoming unintentionally deflated or flat. Constantly grain from your center out to skin surface to fill each shape.

Time

"Time is relentless. It cannot be stopped. The only way to deal with time is to go with it."

Alwin Nikolais

Time is a mystery waiting to be explained. Humans work mightily to define it. We spend time, lose time, waste time, and fill time. A dancer's world is filled with counts, repetitions, holds, starts, arrivals and finales. All the while, we are here, now, breathing and alive. We mark time in measures. We consider when, if, and how long. We experience interruption, the unexpected and the unfinished. We are either present in time or not. It is both a choice and a skill.

To the performer, the uninterrupted flow of presence is the experience and the expression of time. Each moment offers the opportunity to live simultaneously in past, present and future. Mastering the ability to remain fully in the moment requires patience, presence and vision.

Try this:

(1) *Find a comfortable spot to rest, sitting quietly, outdoors or indoors. As you sit, listen to the workings of the world surrounding you. Listen to time passing. Note when you stop listening. How were you spending your time?*

(2) *Begin walking in a specific direction. Continue until your body/mind chooses "when" to change direction. Continue in the new direction and again choose "when" to change direction. Experiment with differing durations of time traveled in each direction. Be sure that you are totally present with each directional change. You can expand this exercise by experimenting with differing walking speeds in each direction. Attune to the moment of transition.*

The Body View:

Stillness is filled with presence as your body listens to the passage of time. The most delicate moments require sustained attention. Active listening, patience and sustained presence open the space of time. Quick, fleeting milliseconds magically flicker into being when you give them life in time and space.

In Performance:

There is an aspect of performing for an audience that could be defined as performance time. It is potent and exists outside the normal intervals we create in our daily lives or sometimes when we rehearse in the studio. Dancers learn to savor it and work to re-create performance time during rehearsal.

When you become accustomed to embodied communication during every moment of a dance, you begin to open the space within time. Consider that you or any dancer can accurately nail a rhythmic phrase. But you still have additional room in time to explore, pull out and stretch that phrase into the full duration of time. This is your opportunity to play within the material and give it resonance.

Being an Instrument

"A foot that smiles, a hand that can weep—well, the dance is not only an art of time and space, it also is the art of the consciously lived and fulfilled moment, not different in the studio from onstage."

Mary Wigman

Dancers' work is extraordinarily hard. You make great sacrifices, often pushing yourself to the point of physical and mental exhaustion. Your body must be trained and maintained. Choreography must be learned, nurtured and refined to the choreographer's vision. Then, you make each dance your own. Partnering and group work requires sustained openness, cooperation and unity of purpose. You learn to see choreography from the inside and the outside. You learn to keep your balance within the charged theatrical environment. You learn to balance your life. Every ounce of your energy is marshaled to give the art its due. You persist. You grow.

Because you are becoming more aware and open, you learn to sense the emotionally physical self in a different way. The sensed qualities of emotion help you navigate and negotiate your way through challenges and breakthroughs to reach higher levels of performance. Presence keeps you from falling back on technique alone. This is not easy—it is tough, personal work.

As you mature as an artist, you imbue your art with the depth of your whole life's experiences. You develop the remarkable ability to experience your body in its fullest expression. As an instrument of dance, you have the opportunity to expand your consciousness to levels that speak to the transformative power of art. Your ability to become what you create is no less than extraordinary. That you communicate the quality of your experience through time and space is equally miraculous.

In the Moment

"The Artist-Me? I don't know him. I've never met him. I know him only when I dance, only when I create, only when I'm alive."

Murray Louis

You have covered a great deal of territory in this small guide. Mastering the expressive performance skills presented here requires you to activate the most facile, daring and creative aspects of your being.

It also takes a great deal of curiosity, practice and commitment to turn your imagination into physical reality. But achieving this transformation—the alchemist's gold of dance performance—is well worth the effort.

When you know a dance by heart, when you are one with it, a most magical window opens into a new reality. The essence of your whole being permeates everything that you create. The act of performance connects this essence, this realization, to the audience's energy and imagination. Through every exertion, every silence, every interaction, every exhilarating instant, you express a greater reality.

You have grown beyond technique and into the realm of presence. Performance moments are the creative realization of all your effort. The space between performer and audience is alive and connected. Within that space lies the power of human expression and communication. It is why you dance. Enjoy the journey.

About the Author

Marcia Wardell Kelly performed in the Murray Louis Dance Company (1970-75) and The Nikolais Dance Theatre (1975 and 1978-81). She has been on the faculty of the Nikolais/Louis Dance Theatre Lab, NY; the Centre National de Danse Contemporaine, Angers, France; The American Dance Festival, Durham, NC; University of California Santa Cruz; University of Minnesota, St. Paul.

Following her performing career, she worked as a dance company manager, court mediator, arts organization administrator, massage therapist, chaplain's assistant, special education advocate, and high school PTA president. She is currently a student of painting, yoga, Buddhist meditation, and Andean indigenous medicine. In recent years, she has renewed her dedication to the art of Dance, creating new choreography and writing this Pocket Guide.

Further Reading

The Nikolais/Louis Dance Technique: A Philosophy and Method of Modern Dance; by Alwin Nikolais and Murray Louis; 2005 Routledge

Inside Dance: Essays by Murray Louis; by Murray Louis; 1980 St. Martin's Press

Big Magic: Creative Living Beyond Fear; by Elizabeth Gilbert; 2015 Riverhead Books Penguin Random House LLC

Touching Enlightenment: Finding Realization in the Body; by Reginald A. Ray, PhD; 2014 Sounds True Inc.

The Brain That Changes Itself: Stories of Personal Triumph from the Frontiers of Brain Science; by Norman Doige, M.D.; 2007 Viking, a member of the Penguin Group

The Mind's Eye; by Oliver Sacks; 2011 Vintage Books

the returns of Alwin Nikolais: bodies, boundaries and the dance canon; by Claudia Gitelman and Randy Martin; 2007 Wesleyan University Press

The Language of Dance; by Mary Wigman; 1966 Wesleyan University Press

The Nikolais/Louis Foundation for Dance: www. nikolaislouis.org

CPSIA information can be obtained
at www.ICGtesting.com
Printed in the USA
BVOW08s2101290817
493373BV00001B/10/P